CHEER UP!

A First-Aid Book for Survivors
By Peter Marshall

Illustrated by Marvin Rubin

 Published by J. P. Tarcher, Inc., Los Angeles

Distributed by Hawthorn Books, Inc., New York

1   2   3   4   5   6   7   8   9   10

Foreword

I have been told that there once was a village in Russia where the people were always complaining of their troubles and misfortunes. Finally, one day the wise man of the village called the people together. When they were gathered in the square, he instructed each of them to write his troubles on a piece of paper and throw the paper in a barrel, which he had placed in the center of the square. This done, he announced that they no longer had their problems.

Needless to say, they cheered him for this brilliant solution. When they stopped, he said, "Of course, these troubles won't simply disappear. Each of you must reach into the barrel and take out a piece of paper — not your own. What is written on that paper will now be your troubles."

One by one the villagers reached into the barrel and took out somebody else's misfortune. When they read what was written on the papers in their hands, they all wanted their own troubles back.

Enough said?

Things moving too fast in your little world?

Cheer up!

Westinghouse calculates that the so-called "half-life" of an engineer is only ten years.

This means that fully one-half of what he learns by the time he graduates from college will be outdated within a decade.

Family meddling in your affairs?

Cheer up!

In the town of Aquina, St. Thomas's brothers locked him in a room and tried to get the village whore to seduce him in order to keep him from going into church work.

Falling behind
in your office work?

Cheer up!

The 1962 Hoang Chinese typewriter has 5850 Chinese characters, a keyboard two feet wide and seventeen inches high.

The fastest that one can type on it is eleven words per minute.

Full denture wearers, all 26 million of you . . .

Cheer up!

. . . there is another way

Mahatma Gandhi had a set of false teeth that he carried in a fold in his loincloth, putting them in his mouth only when he wanted to eat.

After his meal, he'd take them out, wash them carefully and put them back in his loincloth again.

Blondes may have more fun, but . . .

Cheer up!

They don't seem to have it for long.

Not Jayne Mansfield, Marilyn Monroe, Jean Harlow, nor even Marie Antoinette, made it to her 38th birthday.

But then again, if you're a blonde,

Cheer up!

There's one blonde who has proven to be indestructible!

Her secret?

"When I'm good, I'm very good. And when I'm bad, I'm better."
—Mae West (to Cary Grant in *She Done Him Wrong*, 1937)

Swimming upstream?

Cheer up!

You're in good company. Take Abraham Lincoln—

1831   Business failure
1832   Defeated for legislature
1833   Second failure in business
1834   Elected to legislature
1835   Fiancee died
1836   Mental breakdown
1838   Defeated for speaker
1840   Defeated for elector
1843   Defeated for land officer
1843   Defeated for Congress
1846   Elected to Congress
1848   Defeated for Congress
1855   Defeated for Senate
1856   Defeated for vice-president
1858   Defeated for Senate
1860   Elected President

Being combustible, all stars have a limited life.

For instance, our sun has already been burning at least 10 billion years, but

Cheer up!

Although it has less than 10 billion more years to burn, it probably won't go out tomorrow.

Had a business trip where you went round and round in circles?

Cheer up!

Frank Borman
James Lovell
William Anders
Thomas Stafford
Michael Collins
Richard Gordon
John Swigert
Fred Haise
Stuart Roosa
Alfred Warden
Thomas Mattingly
Ronald Evans

. . . all traveled a million miles on trips to the moon and back, but had to mind the command module as it circled and never got to land.

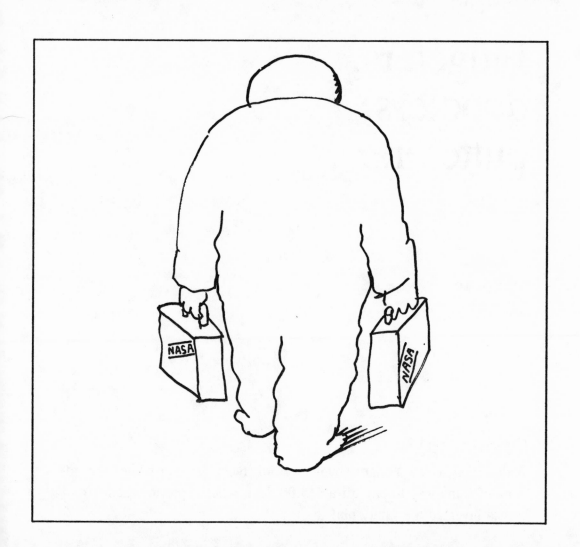

Fidgeters,
doodlers,
putterers,

Cheer up!

Walter Hunt, a New York mechanic, was idly twisting a wire while trying to think of some way to pay off a $15.00 debt, when—presto, change-o— he had invented the safety pin!

Cheer up!
Money
isn't everything . . .

'I wish I had a better personality.' —J. Paul Getty

Are you one of the 40 million Americans who move every year?

In Alvin Toffler's best-selling *Future Shock,* the author outlines a plan for the modular family that will expedite the ever-increasing movement of company executives from place to place.

Under this scheme, the executive not only leaves his house behind, but his family as well. The company then finds him a matching family—complete with personality characteristics carefully selected to duplicate those of the wife and children left behind—at the new site. Some other itinerant executive then "plugs into" the family left behind.

Cheer up!

No one appears to be taking that idea seriously (yet).

The good things
in life seem
to be passing you by
and by
and by?

Cheer up!
Devon Smith, acknowledged to be the world's greatest hitchhiker, on his 6,013th hitch finally got a ride in a Rolls-Royce.

A man named Rod Pack,
one of the nation's top skydivers,
jumped from an airplane
without a parachute not too long ago.
He was handed one in midair
by a companion,
put it on, opened it—and landed
safely.

But cheer up!
You don't have to do that if you don't want to.

How could you
have been so stupid . . . ?

Cheer up!

P. T. Barnum once invested all his money in a scheme to make a "magic preparation" that would grow hair on a bald head. His partner then spent all the money, fled to Europe, and left Barnum with nothing but the recipe!

There's more than one sucker born every minute. . .

"It is our wish and our will
that this state and this realm
may last in the millennia to come.
We may be happy in the
knowledge that
this future is entirely ours."

From a proclamation read before Hitler's speech on the Nazi Party Day, September 5, 1934.

Cheer up!

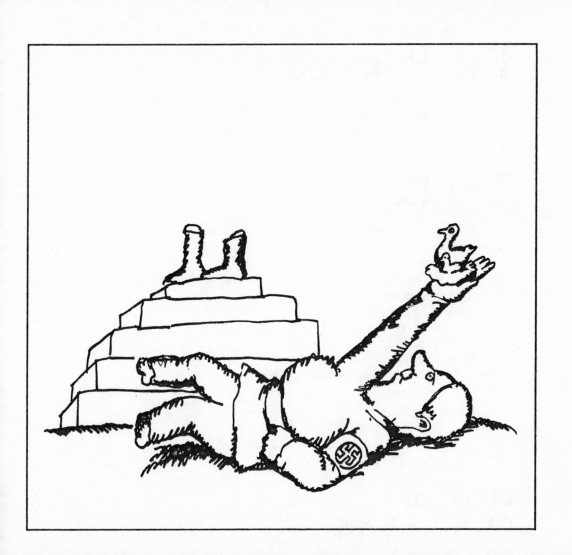

The Promise:

On my honor, I will try:
To do my duty to God and my country,
To help other people at all times,
To obey the Girl Scout Laws.

The Laws:

A Girl Scout's honor is to be trusted.
A Girl Scout is loyal.
A Girl Scout's duty is to be useful and to help others.
A Girl Scout is a friend to all and a sister to every other Girl Scout.
A Girl Scout is courteous.
A Girl Scout is a friend to animals.
A Girl Scout obeys orders.
A Girl Scout is cheerful.
A Girl Scout is thrifty.
A Girl Scout is clean in thought, word, and deed.

Cheer up!

Unless you are a Girl Scout, five out of ten is a passing grade.

If at first you don't succeed,

Cheer up!

Columbus tried for seventeen years to get someone to finance his trip to the New World.

Out of the first four stores F. W. Woolworth opened, three failed. When he died, he was worth more than $20 million.

Admiral Peary tried to reach the North Pole on seven different trips before he made it on the eighth.

Thomas Edison tried 1,600 different materials before settling on carbon as the filament for the electric light bulb.

Oscar Hammerstein II had five flop shows that lasted less than six weeks each before *Oklahoma*—which ran for 2,248 performances (269 weeks) and grossed $7 million on an $83,000 investment.

Willie Mays didn't get a hit in his first 26 times at bat in the Major Leagues. His first hit was a home run off Warren Spahn.

John Creasey, one of the world's most prolific and successful mystery and crime novelists, whose 560 books have sold more than 60,000,000 copies and have been translated into 23 languages, collected 743 rejection slips from publishers before he managed to get a word in print.

Think that your stockbroker is making a fortune while you're losing yours?

Cheer up!

In 1969, seats on the New York Stock Exchange cost $515,000.
In May, 1973, they were selling for $82,000 each.

Thus, the Exchange's 1,366 brokers have suffered a staggering $591,000,000 loss.

Don't get around much any more?

Cheer up!

. . . you're not the only one.

In May of 1973, a Dallas jury recently handed out two 5005-year sentences (even though the district attorney had only asked for 5000-year terms) to Franklin and Woodrow Ransonette, convicted kidnappers.

Off to a bad start?

Cheer up!

In 1963, Stan Smith was turned down for the job of ball boy for the United States Davis Cup team because he was "too clumsy on the court."

In 1973, Stan Smith won the world's professional tennis championship and had over $150,000 in tournament earnings.

Teen-agers!
Think your parents are treating you badly?

Cheer up!

Here's how they treat adolescents in the South Pacific:

The Malekula of the New Hebrides Islands have rites for females to show the passage from girl to woman. Before she can marry, the upper two incisor teeth are knocked out ceremonially, and she then remains secluded in her father's hut for ten days.

The Arunta, nomads of Australia, have a final rite of the passage from boyhood to manhood—the "fire ceremony." The young men have to defend themselves with branches against burning grass and sticks, which the women throw at their heads. Then they must lie down for several minutes on green boughs laid over an open fire. Later they must kneel for a brief moment in the coals of a small fire. At this point, they are considered men in the society.

In Samoa any older relative has the right to demand personal service from younger relatives, and a right to criticize their conduct and to interfere in their affairs.

If you think
that the cost of food on
y<u>our</u> shelf is a burden,

Cheer up!

In order to keep merchandise on their shelves for the year that ended February 24, 1973, the Great Atlantic and Pacific Tea Company—otherwise known as your friendly A&P grocer—suffered a loss of $51,300,000.

Want to simplify your life?

Cheer up!

Albert Einstein has a solution for you.

Einstein would shave while sitting in the bathtub, using the same soap on his face as he did for his bath.

His theory was that using two different kinds of soap tends to make life entirely too complicated.

Relatively.

People constantly pulling the wool over your eyes?

Cheer up!

The curator at the National Gallery of Art recently had to remove eighteen paintings from the museum walls because they turned out to be forgeries;

and a painting by Henri Matisse hung upside down at the Museum of Modern Art in New York for forty-seven days before anyone noticed it.

PORTRAIT OF THE
· CURATOR ·

Recognition slow in coming?

Cheer up!

Once a week for ten years, Robert Ripley drew his *Believe-It-or-Not* cartoon before it became famous when he pointed out that Lindbergh was the sixty-seventh man to fly nonstop across the Atlantic!*

---

*All the others had made the mistake of doing it in groups! *Believe-It-or-Not!*

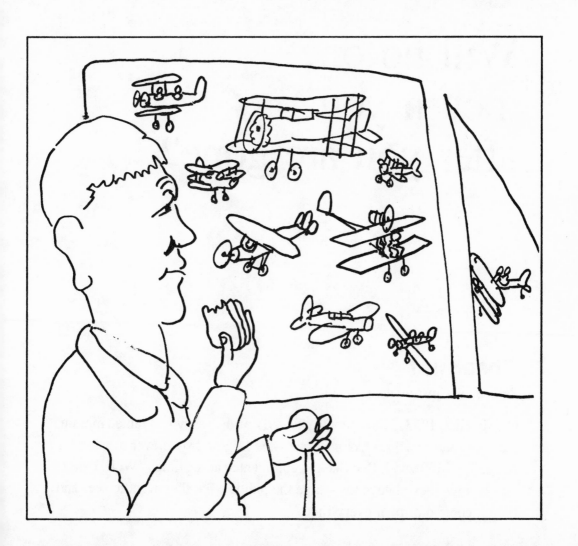

Will no one mourn you after you are gone?

Cheer up!

Perhaps it's just as well.

On March 2, 1958, 2,000 people showed up when they laid famed motion picture producer Harry Cohn to rest—the largest crowd ever to attend a funeral in Hollywood. Red Skelton commented at the time: "Well, it only proves what they always say—give the public what they want to see, and they'll come out for it every time."

Overestimated your future?

Cheer up!

In September of 1972, Teledyne, a Los Angeles-based electronics company, was so positive of its future that it bought almost 9 million shares of its own stock.

Nine months later, Teledyne had a loss on the transaction of more than 70 million dollars.

In describing the situation to a financial analyst, a Teledyne spokesman had a faultless explanation: "What happened, happened."

Hate your name?

Cheer up!

It's easy to change it, and the change may do you good.
It certainly didn't hurt.

Eunice Quedens	Eve Arden	Anthony Benedetto	Tony Bennett
Aaron Chwatt	Red Buttons	Margarita Cansino	Rita Hayworth
Marie van Shaack	Lili St. Cyr	Bernie Schwartz	Tony Curtis
Leonard Slye	Roy Rogers	Benny Kubelsky	Jack Benny
Tula Ellice Finklea	Cyd Charisse	Spangler Arlington Brugh	Robert Taylor
Issur Danielovitch	Kirk Douglas	Archibald Leach	Cary Grant
Frances Gumm	Judy Garland	Izzy Itskowitz	Eddie Cantor
Douglas Ulman	Douglas Fairbanks	Judith Tuvim	Judy Holliday
Arlene Kazanjian	Arlene Francis	Nathan Birnbaum	George Burns
William Beedle	William Holden	Emanuel Goldenberg	Edward G. Robinson
Rose Louise Hovick	Gypsy Rose Lee	Arnold Raymond Cream	Jersey Joe Walcott
Melvin Hesselberg	Melvyn Douglas	Joe L. Barrow	Joe Louis
Dino Crecetti	Dean Martin	Walker Smith	Sugar Ray Robinson
Giovanni de Simone	Johnny Desmond	Doris Mary Anne	
Anna Maria Italiano	Anne Bancroft	Kappelhoff	Doris Day

Hyman Schnicklefritz
Rory Schnicklefritz
Rock Schnicklefritz
Mickey Schnicklefritz
J.J. Schnicklefritz
Buster Schnicklefritz
Bartholomew Schnicklefr

Inconsistent?

Take Wilt Chamberlain . . .
on March 2, 1962,
he set a National Basketball
Association record by scoring one
one hundred points
in a game against New York.

Impressed?

Cheer up!
On March 27, 1973, the very same 7'1" powerhouse,
playing forty-six minutes against Milwaukee, didn't score at all.

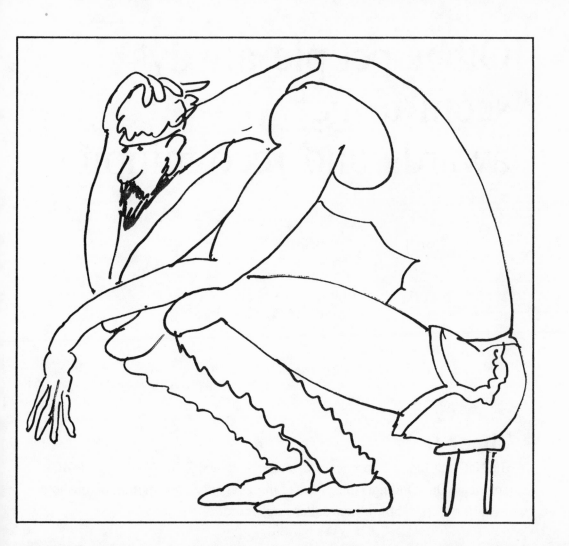

Other people always seem to get awards and recognition?

Cheer up!

The National Junior Chamber of Commerce named Billie Sol Estes one of America's Outstanding Young Men of the Year only a few months before he was arrested in a 50-million-dollar mail fraud.

Struggling songwriters of the world,

Cheer up!

When Cole Porter tried to interest the music publishing world in his beautiful composition, "Night and Day," they turned him down because they were convinced no song whose first note (a B-flat) is repeated thirty-five times in succession could ever make it!*

---

*You know—the part that goes: "With the beat, beat, beat of the tom-toms, when the evening shadows fall . . ."

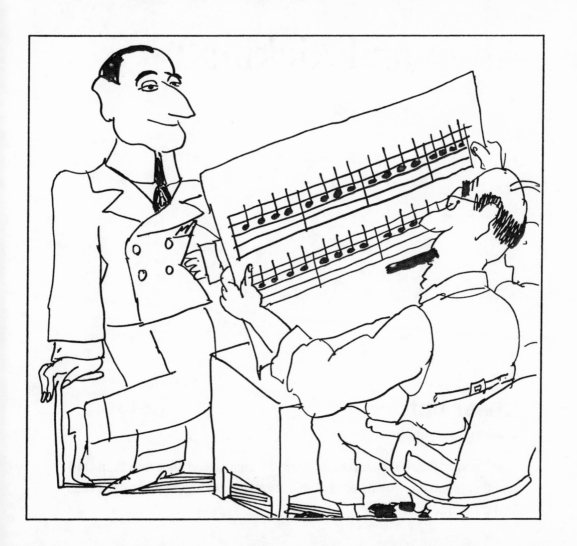

Alive and kicking?

Cheer up!

. . . not everyone is.

The World Health Organization recently announced that one thousand people around the world commit suicide every day, and ten times as many make the attempt.

Christmas card list too long?

Cheer up!

In the United States alone, some 2,248,000,000 Christmas cards are sold every year.

Averaging it out, each adult should receive more than twenty.

Didn't get your share?

Cheer up!

The Post Office lays claim to 8,000,000 undelivered letters from last year.

Does the 429-billion-dollar national debt keep you awake?

Cheer up!

There is a solution!

If each of us went out and borrowed just two grand apiece, we could pay it off overnight.

Ever wish there were two of you? Three? Four?

Cheer up!

. . . and stick around

Scientist and Nobel laureate Joshua Lederberg has suggested that within a mere fifteen years, through a process known as cloning,* man may be able to make *exact biological duplicates of himself*.

---

*A new organism is grown from the nucleus of an adult cell; the organism thus has the same genetic characteristics as the person who contributed the cell nucleus.

Always felt you had a novel in you but knew your efforts wouldn't pay off?

Cheer up!

Peter Benchley, son of Nathaniel and grandson of Robert Benchley, has done pretty well with his first try. In addition to a $250,000 film sale, his first novel has landed $575,000 from Bantam Books for the paperback reprint rights, will be one-half of a dual Book of the Month Club selection, and will be condensed in a *Reader's Digest* volume.

Benchley's personal take from the book before selling one copy: $500,000.

Think you made
a bad deal?

Cheer up!

After years of struggling to find a buyer. Joe Schuster and Jerry Siegel
finally sold to D. C. Comics for $200
all rights to the superhero they had created.

What was the brainchild that brought them this largesse?

It's not a bird . . not a plane . . it's Superman!

More than thirty-five years later, they are still fighting the matter
in the courts.

Bewildered by the opposite sex? Gentlemen . . .

Cheer up!

. . . you're not alone!

"The great question that has never been answered, and which I have not yet been able to answer despite my thirty years of research into the feminine soul, is: What does a woman want?!''—Sigmund Freud

Competition too stiff for you?

Cheer up!

In May, 1504, when Leonardo da Vinci was designing a large painting for the right half of the east wall of the Grand Council Chamber in Florence, Michelangelo was submitting his design for the left half of the wall.

Duffers of the world,

Cheer up!

When Arnold Palmer was asked not too long ago what golf problems, if any, he was having, he replied: "It's the same old story—no confidence in my putting game."

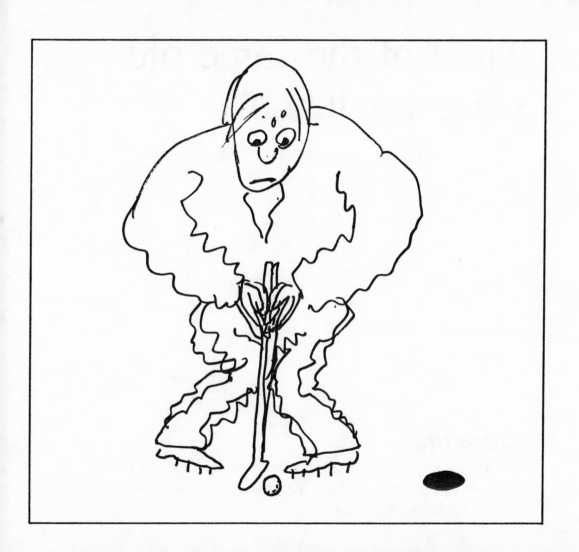

Tired of the same old place for lunch?

Cheer up!

The poorest people in the world live in Australia. There are less than twenty-five Pintibu left, and they have a diet consisting of water from soak holes, rats, lizards, and yams.

Listen, America!

After Nicholas II, the last Czar of Russia, abdicated the throne, he breathed a sigh of relief and murmured: "Thank God. Now I can do what I've always wanted to do. Go home and raise flowers."

And Potemkin, one of Russia's greatest generals, was deathly afraid of guns and used to tremble like a schoolgirl whenever a cannon was fired.

Cheer up!
Maybe the Russians are really just a bunch of sissies.

Can't do anything right?

Cheer up!

In 1885, despite a 250-foot leap from the Clifton suspension bridge in England, the life of jilted Sarah Ann Henley was saved when her voluminous dress and petticoat acted as a parachute and broke her fall.

And in 1972, a Czechoslovakian woman named Vera Czermak was so upset by the news her husband had betrayed her that she tried to commit suicide by leaping from a third-story window. She jumped and landed on her husband, killing him.

American advertising industry researchers have estimated that the average American is assaulted by approximately 540 advertising messages a day, but

Cheer up!
Those same researchers claim that you notice only 76 (more than enough!).

All thumbs?

Cheer up!

So were some of the great ones.

In 1955, John Unitas failed his first pro test with the Pittsburgh Steelers. The first time he took over as quarterback in a regular-season game, he fumbled three times. Each one resulted in a touchdown for the other team. He also threw one interception that went for a touchdown

In the 1970 commemoration of the fiftieth anniversary of the National Football League, Johnny Unitas was selected as the greatest quarterback of all time, and the same year the Associated Press named him the outstanding professional football player of the decade.

Agonizing over the health, sex, features, and future of your unborn baby?

Cheer up!

When it's your own daughter's turn, she may not have to ponder these imponderables. Dr. E. S. E. Hafez, an internationally known biologist from Washington State University, has estimated that within the next twenty years a woman will be able to buy a tiny frozen embryo, have it implanted in he uterus, carry it for nine months, and then give birth to ''her'' baby.

She would thereby know in advance the color of its eyes and hair, its sex its probable size at maturity, and, of course, its probable IQ.

Want to learn a foreign language but don't know where to start?

Cheer up!

You can start anywhere. The first word of English Greta Garbo ever learned was "applesauce"!

Do you think that your business judgment is suspect?

Cheer up!

In 1972—

Boise Cascade
Ampex
Grumman
Collins Radio
National Cash Register
Olin
American Can
Omega-Alpha
Continental Can
Mattel
Ward Foods

—lost a total of more than $687,000,000!

Losing perspective?

Cheer up!

The earth is one of nine planets circling the sun.

The sun is one of 100 billion stars in the Milky Way, our galaxy.

There are at least as many galaxies in the universe as there are stars in the Milky Way.

The light from the spiral galaxy Andromeda (the most distant of all bodies visible to the naked eye) has traveled for 2,200,000 years before reaching the earth.

Andromeda is close compared to a quasar called 4C 05.34, which is 13,000,000,000 light years away.

Light travels 5,878,500,600,000 miles a year.

Therefore, the quasar 4C 05.34 is 76,420,507,800,000,000,000,000 miles from earth, give or take a mile.

Bernard Baruch was one of the few members of the financial community who foresaw the stock crash of 1929.

He sold in time, and while many others were going broke, Baruch made a fortune. The story of his wisdom gained him an enviable reputation, and he lived out his life a wealthy and respected man, the confidant of presidents, but . . .

Cheer up!

He's dead.

This book got you down?

Cheer up!
It's finished!